To:

From:

Aging with Attitude

Better Than Dying with Dignity

Pauline Whitchurch and Evelyn Beilenson

Illustrated by Bonnie Krebs

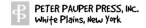
PETER PAUPER PRESS, INC.
White Plains, New York

Designed by Heather Zschock

Illustrations copyright © 2005 Bonnie Krebs

Copyright © 2005
Peter Pauper Press, Inc.
202 Mamaroneck Avenue
White Plains, NY 10601
All rights reserved
ISBN 978-1-59359-976-8
Printed in China

14 13

Visit us at www.peterpauper.com

Ahh . . . those were the days.
Wait a minute . . . they still are!

Aging gracefully? No Way! This bunch of old fogies is storming
into their golden years. Free weights and gym bags have
replaced knitting needles and rocking chairs. And these people
have a great deal to say about life, with the experience to
back it up. So look closely, you're sure to recognize someone—
maybe even yourself—in these hilarious pages.

PAULINE WHITCHURCH

It's not the years . . .
it's the mileage.

Well behaved women seldom make history.

LAUREL THATCHER ULRICH

If you're pushing 50
that's exercise enough.

That skirt does wonders.

When you're hot, you're hot!

If I don't move it,
I'll lose it.

I'm masquerading as a mature adult.

Everything I own
has come
back in style.

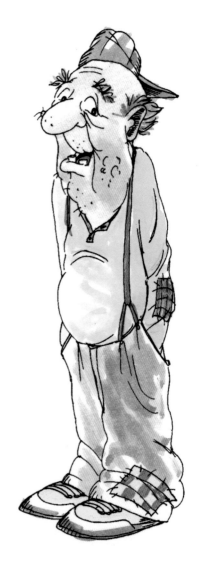

Age isn't important—
it's attitude that counts.

The only thing that needs jogging is my memory.

Let's party 'til
the early bird special.

Independently wealthy widow
seeks "sexy" beast
for a good time.

My wants turned into wents
but that doesn't stop me
from wanting.

Really, what's not to love?

I'm not over the hill;
I'm just enjoying the view.

Along with my gray hair and bifocals I have the wisdom of the ages . . . so bite me!

If the kids insist on these "virtual" visits ... next time I'm sending "virtual" money!

I'm the fitness queen
with a weighty solution
to everything.

I expect to stay
on my toes
as long as possible.

It's garage sales from now on;
I'm livin' la vida broka!

Still do-si-do'n
after all these years.

I'm not old;
I'm chronologically
challenged.

Yes, it *is* always about me.

The upside of senility . . .
getting to embarrass
your children.

We're getting in touch
with our inner child.

Eat your heart out,
Madonna.

I'm the king of cool, waiting for my happenin' babe.

A good-looking dude is still
my cup of tea.

Pick an age you like and stick with it.

We still suit
each other to a tee.

I'm doing a photo shoot for GQ (Geriatric Quarterly).

We think . . . therefore
we know everything.

I didn't invent the good life—
I perfected it.

No need for plastic surgery.
Eat 'til the wrinkles fill in.

I can still light up a room,
as well as four city blocks.

I've still got it;
I just know how to cover it up.

After a night on the town,
there's no place like home.